Martín Raninqueo | *Haikus de guerra*

Martín Raninqueo

War Haikus
Haikus de guerra

Linocuts *by* Julieta Warman

Prologue *by* Leopoldo Brizuela

translated *by* John Oliver Simon

Red Dragonfly Press

Translation copyright © 2016 by John Oliver Simon
Spanish text © 2011 by Martín Raninqueo
  All rights reserved

ISBN 978-1-937693-84-8

Haikus de guerra was originally published in 2011 in La Plata, Argentina as a limited edition at Taller Crisálida (Chrysalis Printshop) by Julieta Warman. Several of the linocuts created for that edition are reproduced here by permission of the artist.

The author wishes to express his gratitude to John Oliver Simon for the opportunity to be translated and published in English.

Designed and typeset by Scott King
  using Dante MT Std, a digital version of

Published by Red Dragonfly Press
  307 Oxford Street
  Northfield, MN 55057
  www.reddragonflypress.org

PROLOGUE

They say that prose is battle. Poetry is the angel that descends, like the gods of the Iliad, to save a wounded hero here and there. The angel that came to the rescue of Martín Raninqueo in the stormy emptiness of the Malvinas [known to English readers as the Falklands], the angel that kept on saving him for 26 years, each time that memory shook out the intolerable shuddering of war, at last that angel speaks to us as well.

The angel's messages are brief. Islands in the sea of the unsayable, missiles thrown against an impersonal black sky that in memory's quietude blossoms with red stars. Haiku from another world that is not so much Japan but the reverse side of England and Argentina. England and Argentina, those monstrous siamese twins of Western Civilization that struggled to devour each other in a process that the language of Martín Raninqueo, a poet who has never evoked the bestial in his commanders and enemies, opposes.

But the angel speaks, and every one of Martín Raninqueo's wounds is healed into a scar on the skin of time. A scar that Julieta Warman has labored to unfold and unpack in linocuts that are translation and revelation, second sight from the field of battle. The angel speaks and goes on speaking. Martín Raninqueo writes and Julieta Warman makes linocuts. They rhyme. Annunciation: someday we will understand.

Two linocuts sewn together by a poem. Others follow, making an enormous tattered cloak: prose and poetry. Some day we'll understand, they say. Here's the proof, in beauty.

– Leopoldo Brizuela

War Haikus

Haikus de guerra

Elegant nasty crow!
on the white tablecloth
of morning

> *Cuervo repelente ¡y airoso!*
> *Sobre el mantel blanco*
> *de la mañana.*

> – Basho

Little islands
between waves' foam
and threads of fog

> *Pequenas islas,*
> *entre la espuma de las olas,*
> *entre los hilos de la niebla*

> – Shoa

Percussion of rain
on the shed roof
(I pretend to read)

Percute la lluvia
el techo del pozo
(Hago que leo)

cold night
I hope she's dreaming I'm
asleep at her side

noche de frío
(que ella me sueñe
a su lado tendido)

No one in sight
except for the wind
playing with a bucket

Nadie a la vista
salvo el viento
jugando con una olla

Hillside sheep
from a distance resemble
flocks of clouds

Ovejas del monte
de lejos parecen
rebaños de nubes

The wind is sweet
when it carries snowflakes
rather than screams

Dulce es el viento
si no arrastra gritos
y esparce la nieve

(in the trenches)

Over the crowd of us
a single green branch
dying of cold

      (el estaqueo)

      Sobre la turba
      ramita verde
      muriéndose de frío

Sun hits the mountain
we sing the National Anthem
(feigning courage)

Sol en el monte
Cantamos el Himno
(fingimos coraje)

Nobody in sight
except the fog
slowly erasing Mount Longdon

Nadie a la vista
salvo la niebla
que está borrando el Longdon

Mount Longdon, the high ground overlooking Port Stanley, was the site of a crucial battle (British victory, Argentine defeat) in the Falklands War.

fireflies of death
arriving at dusk
they come from the sea

luciérnagas de muerte
llegando el ocaso
vienen del mar

a gust of wind
gives a shove to a soldier
wounded on the hillside

brusco es el viento
que empuja a un soldado
herido en el monte

Frozen afternoon
when the mortar hesitates
the silence deafens

Helada tarde
Aturde el silencio
si duda el mortero

Flake upon frozen flake
Red drops are dripping
(one after another)

Copos sobre copos
Caen gotas rojas
(una tras otra)

Roar, rifle!
Celebrate with us
the end of the war

¡Brama, fusil!
Festeja con nosotros
el fin de la guerra

Sleet and sadness
transported to H. M. S. Canberra
on the high seas

Ventisca y tristeza
Camino al Canberra
que está en alta mar

Argentine soldiers, mostly young conscripts like the author, were held as P. O.W.'s for a time on victorious British naval vessels.

Beyond the mist
the kids we used to be
are screaming at us goodbye

Tras la bruma
los niños que fuimos
nos están gritando adios

Martín Raninqueo is an Argentine Native American poet and musician whose surname derives from his Mapuche great-grandfather. He was born in La Plata in June 1962 and was conscripted in 1982, along with many young men of his generation, to fight against the British expeditionary force in Las Malvinas (Falkland Islands). He was held as a prisoner of war aboard the HMS Canberra. The loss of that war brought an end to the miltary junta that was responsible for the disappearance of over 30,000 dissidents and their families. As a musician, Martín Raninqueo has released numerous CD's both solo and with other artists.

Julieta Warman was born in 1975 in the city of La Plata, Buenos Aires. She is a teacher of Fine Arts, graduating from the National University of La Plata.

Leopoldo Brizuela is an Argentine writer and translator. Born in La Plata in 1963, he has won a number of literary awards, including the 2012 Premio Alfaguara for his novel *Una misma noche*. As a translator, he has translated the works of American writers such as Henry James, Flannery O'Connor and Eudora Welty into Spanish.

John Oliver Simon is a poet and translator specializing in contemporary Latin American poetry. His cultural reporting has been featured in *Poetry Flash* and *American Poetry Review*. In 1989 Simon was awarded an Individual Artist's Fellowship by the California Arts Council. He also received an NEA Fellowship in Translation for his work with the great Chilean surrealist poet Gonzalo Rojas (1917-2011).

www.ingramcontent.com/pod-product-compliance
Lightning Source LLC
Chambersburg PA
CBHW031943070426
42450CB00006BA/868